S0-AZS-786

The Parish as a School of Prayer

Foundations for the New Evangelization

Father Scott Traynor, JCL

THE INSTITUTE FOR PRIESTLY FORMATION
IPF PUBLICATIONS

NIHIL OBSTAT: Father Matthew J. Gutowski, STL

IMPRIMATUR: Most Reverend George J. Lucas
Archbishop of Omaha, Neb.
January 18, 2013

THE INSTITUTE FOR PRIESTLY FORMATION
IPF PUBLICATIONS
2500 California Plaza
Omaha, NE
www.priestlyformation.org

Printed in the United States of America
ISBN-13: 978-0-9843792-9-3
ISBN-10: 0-9843792-9-0

Book design by FAITH Catholic Publishing and Communications,
Lansing, Mich.

The Institute for Priestly Formation

Mission Statement

The Institute for Priestly Formation was founded to assist bishops
in the spiritual formation of diocesan seminarians and priests in the
Roman Catholic Church. The Institute responds to the need to foster
spiritual formation as the integrating and governing principle of all
aspects for priestly formation. Inspired by the biblical-evangelical
spirituality of Ignatius Loyola, this spiritual formation has as its
goal the cultivation of a deep interior communion with Christ; from
such communion, the priest shares in Christ's own pastoral charity.
In carrying out its mission, the Institute directly serves diocesan
seminarians and priests as well as those who are responsible for
diocesan priestly formation.

The Institute for Priestly Formation
Creighton University
2500 California Plaza
Omaha, NE 68178
www.priestlyformation.org
ipf@creighton.edu

Table of Contents

7   Foreword

9   Introduction

11   Chapter 1:
The Urgent Need for
Parishes To Become
Genuine Schools of Prayer

19   Chapter 2:
The Curriculum
of the School of Prayer

45   Chapter 3:
Classrooms for the
School of Prayer

55   Chapter 4:
Simple Plans for Prayer

61   Endnotes

Foreword

While I was discussing with a seminarian the possible parishes to which he could be assigned for his last year of seminary formation, he revealed to me that he had a particular parish he strongly preferred. I asked him, "Why that parish?" Without hesitating, he said, "Because when I go to that parish for Sunday Mass, I can tell that the people in that parish really pray. The pastor of that parish is teaching the people how to pray, and I want to learn how to do that." After hearing that, I wanted to assign all the seminarians to that priest and parish!

If you are a pastor who has the same noble desire as that seminarian, then keep reading. *The Parish as a School of Prayer* will meet that desire. If you are a pastor who is trying to write a parish mission statement with just the right words that succinctly express the purpose and mission of your parish, you can stop writing. *The Parish as a School of Prayer* is a parish mission statement — that is more meaningful than any I have read. If you are a pastor who is looking for helpful reading material to give the members of your parish staff and councils, you can stop looking. You are holding it in your hands. *The Parish as a School of Prayer* not only will assist pastors, but will greatly benefit those who support pastors in carrying out the mission of a parish. It is written in an accessible language that all can understand.

Drawing from the *Catechism of the Catholic Church*, Blessed John Paul II, and Pope Benedict XVI as his primary sources, Father Scott Traynor holds up with exciting clarity a vision of parish life that is ever ancient and ever new: the parish as a school of prayer. The parish is the school; the pastor is the teacher; and the encounter between man and God — prayer — is the subject taught. It is a vision that is guaranteed to encourage the priestly heart of any pastor who has gotten bogged down in projects, programs, and committees.

The most needed credential to be a teacher in this privileged school is to know Jesus. Father Traynor does. *The Parish as a School of Prayer* is filled with lived wisdom from his wide experience as a pastor, spiritual director, seminary formator, spiritual theology instructor, and personal friend of Christ. He can be trusted. So, believe what you read; teach what you believe; and practice what you teach!

Father Thomas Richter
Rector, Cathedral of the Holy Spirit
Diocese of Bismarck, N.D.

Introduction

Is your parish a genuine school of prayer? What does it mean for a parish to be a "school of prayer"? It was Blessed John Paul II himself who urged priests to transform their parishes into powerhouses of prayer.

Our Christian communities must become genuine "schools" of prayer, where the meeting with Christ is expressed not just in imploring help but also in thanksgiving, praise, adoration, contemplation, listening and ardent devotion, until the heart truly "falls in love." Intense prayer, yes, but it does not distract us from our commitment to history: by opening our heart to the love of God it also opens it to the love of our brothers and sisters, and makes us capable of shaping history according to God's plan .... [I]t would be wrong to think that ordinary Christians can be content with a shallow prayer that is unable to fill their whole life. Especially in the face of the many trials to which today's world subjects faith, they would be not only mediocre Christians but "Christians at risk." They would run the insidious risk of seeing their faith progressively undermined, and would perhaps end up succumbing to the allure of "substitutes," accepting alternative religious proposals and even indulging in far-fetched superstitions .... It is therefore essential that education in prayer should become in some way a key-point of all pastoral planning.[1]

What is in the urgency of that "must" become schools of prayer? Is it really possible that prayer be a "key-point of all pastoral planning"? How can a priest respond to this exhortation in practical and effective ways?

chapter 1

The Urgent Need
for Parishes To Become Genuine Schools of Prayer

Agony in the Garden by Andrea Mantagna

Why "must" our parishes become genuine schools of prayer? Blessed John Paul II offers the reasons. The world today poses many hazards that are capable of progressively undermining faith. Secularism, relativism,[2] materialism, narcissism, and a "culture of distraction"[3] all hinder a deep and growing intimacy in faith with the Father, Son, and Holy Spirit. These cultural currents hold forth empty substitutes to the human heart, which is made for God — a heart that remains restless until it rests in God alone.[4] Lacking real, daily, and growing intimacy with God in prayer deprives the Christian of the lived experience of Divine Love. Divine Love alone is capable of inspiring, directing, and sustaining the Christian's mission to transform culture according to God's plan. "I am the vine, you are the branches. Whoever remains in me and I in him will bear much fruit, because without me you can do nothing" (Jn 15:5). Christians are at risk precisely because they do not know how to remain in Christ in the growing intimacy of prayer. Christians who do not pray can do nothing to shape their life, their family, or the world according to God's plan of love. Conversely, the praying Christian can do so abundantly and fruitfully.

The risk that the Holy Father points out is clearly realized in parishes today. Would Sunday Mass attendance really stand at 30 percent if people were learning to pray in such a way that their hearts truly fell in love with God? How many families have led other families to faith in Christ and His Church? Indeed, how many parents and grandparents who at least valued the faith are untouched by the sadness of children and grandchildren who no longer practice the faith in any discernible way? How many parishioners (and priests!) seek their happiness, their strength, their security, their comfort, and their peace from God first of all? How many have evaded the allure of empty substitutes (accomplishment, notoriety, possessions, entertainment) or even far-fetched superstitions? How many experience an intimacy with God that is real and deep enough to sustain them in the face of a cancer diagnosis, or the death of a child, or a betrayal, or the loss of a job, or even ordinary everyday difficulties, disappointments, and failures? How many go beyond superficial and occasional recitations of prayer, such as Grace before meals, an occasional Our Father, or a Hail Mary before going to sleep? How often do parishioners go beyond "a shallow prayer that is unable to fill their whole life?"[5] If not many, then our parishes are full of Christians at risk.

THE PRIEST AS THE MASTER TEACHER OF PRAYER

Leading the parish to become a school of prayer, resolving that "education in prayer should become a key-point in all pastoral planning,"[6] is the remedy for the heart-sickness of Christians at risk. Every school needs a master teacher capable of teaching others to teach. Happily, God provides such a master teacher in every parish so it may become a genuine school of prayer — the priest!

Both Blessed John Paul II and Pope Benedict XVI set forth this encouragement: "Your first duty as pastors is not projects and organizations, but to lead your people to a deep intimacy with the Trinity."[7] It is the *first* duty of pastors. It is not reserved to those with a special interest or acumen. It is a *primary* responsibility of the priest. Pope Benedict, for his part, gives voice to the rightful expectation of the faithful founded on this responsibility: "The faithful expect only one thing from priests: that they be specialists in promoting the encounter between man and God. The priest is not asked to be an expert in economics, construction or politics. He is expected to be an expert in the spiritual life."[8] Similarly, seminary formation is to develop the future priest's capacity to fulfill his responsibility and the expectations of the faithful. "Spiritual formation …

should be conducted in such a way that the students may learn to live in intimate and unceasing union with God the Father through his Son Jesus Christ, in the Holy Spirit. Those who are to take on the likeness of Christ the priest by sacred ordination should form the habit of drawing close to him as friends in every detail of their lives. They should live his paschal mystery in such a way that they will know *how to initiate into it the people committed to their charge*."[9]

When confronted with the call and responsibility to be the master teacher of his parish, the school of prayer, a priest may well object: "I was not formed in this way. I am far from living in intimate and unceasing union with God. I have poor habits of drawing close to Christ in every detail of my life. I have little idea how to initiate others into deep intimacy with the Trinity. And if I offered a class on prayer, how many would even bother to show up?" Yet, the call and the responsibility remain.[10]

Pope Benedict addresses this sense of alarm that can fill the priest's heart: "We can be tempted to cry out with Peter: 'Lord, depart from me, for I am a sinful man' (**Lk 5:8**), because we find it hard to believe that Christ called us specifically. Could he not have chosen someone else, more capable, more holy? But Jesus has looked lovingly upon each one of us, and in this gaze of his we may have confidence."[11]

If the priest will honestly acknowledge and entrust to God any doubt, insecurity, indifference, ambivalence, fear, or anxiety which arises in his heart as he is called to be a master teacher of prayer, forming his parish as a school of prayer, he will be met by the loving gaze of Jesus. If he chooses to receive that loving gaze and remain in it, he will find the confidence, courage, wisdom, understanding, desire, and inspiration necessary to offer a generous, fruitful, and effective "Yes" to the call. Pope Benedict XVI again states:

Believe in the power of your priesthood! By virtue of the sacrament, you have received all that you are. When you utter the words "I" and "my" ("I absolve you ... This is my body ..."), you do it not in your own name, but in the name of Christ, "in persona Christi", who wants to use your lips and your hands, your spirit of sacrifice and your talent. At the moment of your ordination, through the liturgical sign of the imposition of hands, Christ took you under his special protection; you are concealed under his hands and in his Heart. Immerse yourselves in his love, and give him your love! When your hands were anointed with oil, the sign of the Holy Spirit, they were destined to serve the Lord as his own hands in today's world.[12]

As a priest for 55 years, head of the Congregation for the Doctrine of the Faith for 25 years, and pope for one year, Benedict XVI was not naïve about the sinfulness, frailty, and limitations of priests as he gave this address. Yet, one can hear his confidence. It is a confidence born of his own choosing to receive the loving gaze of Jesus precisely in the face of such daunting realities.

Master, Teach Us to Pray

Parishioners will never put forth the effort to engage in the "battle of prayer"[13] if their desire to pray is not awakened. For Christians at risk, this desire may be weak or dead. It must be strengthened or even resurrected before they will be willing to receive formation in prayer. "He was praying in a certain place, and when he had finished, one of his disciples said to him, 'Lord, teach us to pray ...'" **(Lk 11:1)**. What prompted this request? What was it that awoke the disciple's desire to learn to pray as Jesus prayed? It is Jesus' deep communion with the Father,[14] fostered in prayer and manifested in all He says and does,[15] that awakens the disciple's desire to learn to pray. When children witness the intimacy of their parents, perhaps, in a heart-to-heart conversation in the living room, or Mom and Dad slow dancing in the kitchen, they naturally want to enter into that intimacy. They jump up on the couch, or grab the dancing legs — not to interrupt, but to be welcomed into the intimacy. The Disciples behold the intimacy Jesus has with the Father and that stirs their desire to learn to pray. "In seeing the Master at prayer, the disciple of Christ also wants to pray. By *contemplating* and hearing the Son, the master of prayer, the children learn to pray to the Father."[16]

To awaken the desire to pray in his parishioners, the priest himself must cultivate a real and growing intimacy with the Father, Son, and Holy Spirit.

> *First, the pastor ought to make the call to his parish to enter a life of prayer from out of his own spiritual conversion, one that has marked his identity and ministry. At minimum the call ought to emerge from his own desire to deepen whatever level of intimacy his prayer life has achieved thus far in his priestly life. The authenticity of the call, and the passion which commits the pastor to make this call continual, and not episodic, will be key to the success of creating parishes as schools of prayer. This does not mean that the pastor teaches or preaches in an autobiographical manner. Rather, he draws his passion to teach about the saints' prayer or liturgical prayer or lectio divina from the power of his own conversion. He draws attention not to himself but to the interior life and its fruits.[17]*

The priest must become a Christian witness of prayer. A professor says, "This is the truth." A witness says, "This is the truth, and this is how it has made a real difference for me." A Christian witness says, "This is the truth; this is how it has made all the difference for me, and, because I love you, I want you to experience the goodness I have been blessed to receive." The priest, as the master teacher of prayer, a Christian witness of prayer, is never in the position of being a "guru." He does not draw attention to himself, but to the utter necessity, goodness, and beauty of deepening intimacy with God in prayer. In union with Jesus, who is meek and humble of heart, in union with Jesus, who is the revelation of the Father's love, the priest witnesses to God's faithful initiative of love and invites, encourages, and assists his parishioners to receive and respond to that love in prayer. The more the priest knows himself to be a beloved son of the Father and a priest of Jesus Christ on the basis of a deepening experience of divine love in prayer, and the more his ministerial activity flows from this love-filled identity, the more authentic, passionate, continual, and powerful the call to prayer for the parish will be.

In calling the parish to the life of prayer, the priest is uniting himself with God's own loving initiative. "*God calls man first.* Man may forget his Creator or hide far from his face; he may run after idols or accuse the deity of having abandoned him; yet the living and true God tirelessly calls each person to that mysterious encounter known as prayer. In prayer, the faithful God's initiative of love always comes first; our own first step is always a response."[18]

In saying "Yes" to cultivating his own habit of daily relational prayer, the priest is offering an obedient "Yes" to God's loving initiative and is humbly acknowledging that, apart from Jesus, he can do nothing.[19] In the face of many demands for his time, attention, and effort for good things, the priest's personal prayer can easily take a back seat. "Let us not be consumed with haste, as if time dedicated to Christ in silent prayer were time wasted. On the contrary, it is precisely then that the most wonderful fruits of pastoral service come to birth… Be assiduous in the prayer of adoration, and teach it to the faithful."[20] Similarly, "generous self-giving for others is impossible without discipline and constant recovery of true faith-filled interiority. The effectiveness of pastoral action depends, ultimately, upon prayer; otherwise, service becomes empty activism. Therefore the time spent in direct encounter with God in prayer can rightly be described as the pastoral priority *par excellence*: it is the soul's breath, without which the priest necessarily remains 'breathless,' deprived of the 'oxygen' of optimism and joy, which he needs if he is to allow himself to be sent, day by day, as a worker into the Lord's harvest. Amen!"[21]

QUESTIONS FOR REFLECTION

1. What spiritual needs does my parish family have? How would a growing habit of daily relational prayer among members of the parish impact those needs?

2. What stirs in my heart when I hear the Church's call for the priest to be the master teacher of prayer in the parish? Have I related these thoughts, feelings, and desires to God in my own prayer? What happens when I do?

3. What difficulties do I experience when I make efforts to pray? Who can I look to for help and encouragement in prayer? Are there other people in my daily life I can encourage and assist in their efforts to pray?

chapter 2

The Curriculum of the School of Prayer

The Pietà by Enguerrand Charonton

For the priest who hears the call to form his parish as a school of prayer, who becomes aware of the urgent need to act on that call, who humbly trusts in God's grace to take on the mantle of being the master teacher of prayer for his people, and who begins to see the awakening of a desire for prayer in his parishioners — such a priest confronts a couple of very practical questions: "Where do I begin?" "What is the curriculum of this school of prayer?" In this chapter, we will look at four essential habits of relational prayer and address several special topics that are of great value for people who are beginning to learn how to pray. This is the core curriculum of the school of prayer.

THE CORE CURRICULUM: FOUR ESSENTIAL HABITS OF PRAYER

When priests and seminarians come to various programs of The Institute for Priestly Formation, they very soon encounter the acronym ARRR — Acknowledge, Relate, Receive, Respond. These four habits of interiority are the essential dynamics of growing Trinitarian intimacy. We will consider what each habit means and how they are all mutually interdependent.

Acknowledge

Prayer is a relationship. It is a personal relationship of growing intimacy with the Father, Son, and Holy Spirit. It is a dialogue of love.[22] Like any relationship, intimacy with God grows as I come to know and love Him and as I experience being known and loved by Him. This mutual knowing and loving is predicated on the relational commitment of self-revelation, which is only possible if I am self-aware. In order to receive the gift of greater intimacy with God, I must first become aware of what is transpiring in my heart.[23] When I glance interiorly to notice what is transpiring in my heart, I find three sorts of things: thoughts, feelings, and desires. These thoughts, feelings, and desires are either connected to my present experience or to my remembered experience.

The first essential habit of relational prayer is to acknowledge (notice, see, name, attend to, become aware of) the thoughts, feelings, and desires that are moving in my heart. The person praying wants to notice — not analyze, critique, prioritize, judge or filter, but simply notice — what is happening in his heart. This is a contemplative noticing, a gazing with love upon what is there: the good, the bad, and the ugly; the significant and the trivial; the noble and the petty; the excellent and the messed-up.

While this noticing is simple, it is not necessarily easy. If someone asks me what is on my mind today, I can stop, think a moment, and respond. But very likely, I will need to stop and think. We are not in the habit of attending to our thoughts, feelings, and desires. Furthermore, we live in a culture of distraction, which continually draws us to attend to the external and ignore the internal.[24] We all the more easily follow, or even seek, such diversion when what we find moving in our heart is painful, difficult, frightening, overwhelming, or ugly. If I deem my heart to be a treacherous place, I am not motivated to gaze upon it.

What is in our heart is very important — not because of some sentimental reason, but because our thoughts, feelings, and desires shape our actions. "But what comes out of a person, that is what defiles. From within people, from their hearts, come evil thoughts, unchastity, theft, murder, adultery, greed, malice, deceit, licentiousness, envy, blasphemy, arrogance, folly. All these evils come from within and they defile" (**Mk 7:20-23**).

To be sure, not every thought, feeling, and desire is spiritually significant; but the activity of the good spirit and evil spirit[25] is concentrated on the battlefield of each human heart. Like a soldier rendered deaf and blind in the midst of battle, the Christian who fails to cultivate a habitual awareness of the movements of his heart is a Christian at risk.

Relate

To say that the first essential habit of relational prayer is to acknowledge my thoughts, feelings, and desires is by no means saying that prayer is an exercise in introspection alone, that it is a kind of narcissistic self-absorption.[26] The second essential habit of prayer is to gather what is in my heart and honestly *relate* it to God, to tell God all about it, to talk to the Father, Son, and Holy Spirit about what is found in my heart, to entrust what is in my heart to God.

Doing so seems like a small thing, but it is a huge interior leap. I am not accustomed to walking into a pitch-black room and beginning to chat about my day on the off-chance that someone might be there to listen.[27] In order to relate what is in my heart to God, I must be aware, in faith, that God is present, that He listens, that He sees, that He cares and takes interest in me. In short, the act of entrusting what I find in my heart to God is an act of faith in His love for me and disposes my heart to receive a greater lived experience of that love.

The fact that God knows me better than I know myself does not absolve me from the reality of intimacy that is founded on a mutual commitment of self-revelation. God invites us to intimacy; He does not force intimacy upon us. Yes, God does know us better than we know ourselves, yet Jesus asks the blind man, "What do you want me to do for you?" (Mk 10:51) He asks the Disciples on the road to Emmaus, "What are you discussing as you walk along?" (Lk 24:17) He commands us to ask, to seek, and to knock (Mt 7:7), to entrust our desires to Him. God does not need the news update. He invites us to relate our thoughts, feelings, and desires to Him because, as our Creator, He knows this disposes our hearts to receive everything He desires to give us.

Think of a dad whose son is playing basketball in high school. The team happens to be coached by a good friend of the dad. Dad, who never misses a game when he is in town, cannot be at Thursday night's game because he is away on a business trip. His son is the star of the game — stealing the ball and sinking a game-winning basket from five feet beyond the three-point line as the buzzer sounds. The coach is so excited he calls Dad on the way home from the game and tells him all about his son's heroics. Dad flies home on Friday; and when his son comes home from school, says to him, "Hey, tell me about the game last night." Why? Dad already knows everything that happened; the coach already told him the story. More importantly, though, it is a loving thing for the dad to ask his son. He wants to hear the story from his son, to listen to his son's heart. He wants his son to know his interest in him. To ask his son to share his experience is an expression of love on the part of the dad. The desire to be attentive to his beloved son's experience springs from the dad's love. When the son agrees and tells his dad the story, his relating is an expression of love to his dad. The communion of love between them deepens. The son's heart becomes especially receptive to his dad's pride, affection, and encouragement in a way it never would have if dad had just said, "Hey, coach told me you were the star last night; way to go."

Receive

To generously receive and stay with the grace of God is the third essential habit of growing intimacy with the Father, Son, and Holy Spirit.

Why does Jesus command us to seek, to knock, and to ask? Why, when the Disciples ask Him to teach them to pray, does

Jesus reply with the seven petitions of the Our Father? Because in relationship with God, we always are in a position of receptivity. We depend completely on God for every good thing. He created us from nothing and sustains us in being at every moment. "Recognizing this utter dependence with respect to the Creator is a source of wisdom and freedom, of joy and confidence."[28] To live according to this truth is to imitate Jesus. Jesus does nothing on His own. All of His words and works come from the Father and reveal the truth that He is the beloved Son, and that the Father and He are one.[29] Receptivity to God's love is fruitful. Indeed, "The most fruitful activity of the human person is to be able to receive God."[30] At the Annunciation, Mary does not say, "I'll do it"; she says, "Let it be done to me." The opposite of total dependence on God is some form of self-sufficiency. To live in an illusion of self-sufficiency is the cause of foolishness, slavery, sorrow, and insecurity.

It is difficult for us to believe that living in dependence on and receptivity to God is especially pleasing to Him. We would much rather do something great for God to "earn" His love. The truth is that God's love for us is gratuitous and unconditional. That we can do nothing to cause God to love us or to stop loving us runs afoul of some deeply held lie in our hearts. God stubbornly resists this lie.

Following is an example that helps to illustrate the relationship between God and mankind: A young boy gets it in his head to give his mom a bouquet of flowers. Fortunately, there is an ample supply of lovely yellow ones available as far as the eye can see — dandelions. So, he gathers them up and proudly presents them to Mom. And how does Mom respond? Does she scold her son and tell him to get those lousy weeds out of her house? Of course not. She takes the dandelions, puts them in a glass of water or a little vase and places them on the kitchen table, or the windowsill above the kitchen sink. Then, she says to her son,

"Thank you," and "They're beautiful," and "I love you, too."

Why does the mother respond in such a way to the gift of the "flowers"? They are, in fact, weeds. But Mom knows her son is simply loving her. Her son is giving a gift, which is an expression of love; and when we love, we give our very selves. Mom knows that her little boy has infused this poor sign — the dandelion — with something very precious, indeed, the love of his heart. And so, Mom cherishes the gift with care and attention, like she cherished her son when he was first born and placed in her arms. And while she may use the words, "Thank you; they're beautiful; I love you, too," by her generous receiving of the gift, she also communicates something else very important. By her receptivity, she says to her son, even without words, "I want to receive more of you."

This familiar exchange is an icon of our relationship with God. But who is who in the exchange? We can easily see ourselves as that little boy. We would really like to do something great for God, to give him three dozen long-stem roses of deep prayer, heroic virtue, and a holy life. However, with all our sins, our flaws, and our failings, it seems our efforts at being prayerful and charitable and devout amount to so many dandelions.

In the story of the boy and the mother, one might think that God is like the mother and that we are as the child, seeking God's appreciation. This interpretation is exactly backwards. It is God who comes to us in the distressing poverty of a little child. He takes simple, ordinary daily realities and pours His very self into them. Think of the Eucharist. Here is a tiny unleavened wafer and some cheap wine, and Jesus so completely pours Himself out in love that they, in reality, become Him: Body, Blood, Soul, and Divinity. And this manifestation is happening all the time in every aspect of creation. God is making Himself present, laboring to communicate His love.[31] So, how can we communicate to God, "Thank you; you are beautiful; I love you, too, and I want to receive more of you"? We say all of that perfectly, even without words, when we generously *receive* the tangible expression of God's love.

What are these tangible expressions, these dandelions God offers to us? They might be words of Scripture that bring comfort or encouragement that we hold in our heart throughout the day. They might be the consoling memories of a blessing we received years ago. They might be words of counsel from a trusted friend that carry the wisdom of God. Or they might be an awareness of the majesty of God stirred by a beautiful sunset. When we place these divine dandelions on the table of our heart and glance at them throughout the day, we are generously receiving God's love for us.

God's love for us is infinite and eternal, but our hearts are finite and limited; they cannot contain the infinite and eternal love of God. God knows this and overcomes our limits by communicating His love in such a way that we can offer a true "Yes" and authentically receive that love. Divine dandelions are like Trojan horses of God's love. God scales His love, without diminishing it, to something that can "fit" in our hearts today. If we will generously receive the particular grace, mysteriously, the whole of God's love will be communicated, and our heart's capacity to receive love will expand. This is why God gives us life each day, that we may grow in our capacity to receive His Love.

The most important question to be able to answer in a concrete, specific, personal way at any moment is, "How is God loving me right now?" This is our anchor. Without it, we are adrift amid forces around us and within us that are incomprehensible. The particular, personal love of God for us in this moment is our life, our existence, and our all. Apart from this love, we are nothing and can do nothing. But, as we grow in the habit of receiving the particular graces God gives, we readily grow into the full stature of Christ and become more and more authentically the unique and unrepeatable persons God has made us to be.[32]

Respond

The grace we receive from God calls for a response. What does God ask of the one He loves? "'Teacher, which commandment in the law is the greatest?' He said to him, 'You shall love the Lord, your God, with all your heart, with all your soul, and with all your mind. This is the greatest and the first commandment. The second is like it: You shall love your neighbor as yourself. The whole law and the prophets depend on these two commandments'" **(Mt 22:36-40)**.

Our response to God, loving Him and loving our neighbor for His sake, always is the result of having generously received His love for us. "In this is love: not that we have loved God, but that he loved us and sent his Son as expiation for our sins. Beloved, if God so loved us, we also must love one another.... We love because he first loved us" **(1 Jn 4:10-11, 19)**.

When we grow in the habit of receiving, resting in, and saying "Yes" to the particular experience of God's love that is available to us at a given moment, that very grace will inspire, direct, and sustain a concrete and particular response of love.

Imagine a sailboat. What factors determine its direction and speed? There are several: the force and direction of the wind, the size and shape of the sail, the position of the rudder, the shape of the hull, the current and the wave state, to name a few. All of these dynamic factors combine to establish the specific direction and speed of the boat at any given moment. Now, imagine a super-intelligent wind that knows the boat's destination and the exact time it needs to arrive. This super-intelligent wind is capable of accounting for all the variables impacting the boat's heading and speed, and then approaches the boat from the exact direction with the exact force which will, if it is fully received in the sail, propel the boat in such a way that it will arrive at its destination precisely on time.

We are the boat; our hearts are the sail, and the super-intelligent wind is the Holy Spirit, the *ruah*. If we generously receive the Holy Spirit in the particular way He comes to us, He will account for all the factors that are impacting us in the present moment and propel us in the particular way God is calling us to love. When we receive the particular expression of God's love for us in the present moment, that love will crystallize into grace-filled inspiration to love in concrete ways. The response that God asks of us is inspired, directed, and sustained by the very grace He has given, if the grace is generously received. A sailboat cannot run up the sail, catch the wind, and then hope to use that energy five hours later. The capturing (receiving) of the wind propels the movement of the boat (the response). They are inseparable realities. If a sailboat is not receiving the wind, the sailboat is just drifting; it has no power to do anything. We are sailboats; our hearts are the sails, and God's love is the wind. We are called to receive the love of God and then to make all of our decisions from out of our communion with Divine Love.

THE INTERDEPENDENCE OF ACKNOWLEDGE, RELATE, RECEIVE, RESPOND

It is very important to stress that to Acknowledge, Relate, Receive, and Respond (ARRR) is not a *method* of prayer. If I am praying for an hour, I do not sit down and acknowledge my thoughts, feelings, and desires for 15 minutes, tell God all about them for 15 minutes, receive His love for 15 minutes, and respond in some way for 15 minutes. Rather, these are four essential interior habits to deepen my relationship with God in times of prayer and throughout my day. They are relational dynamics of growing, Trinitarian intimacy that must be present in any authentic method of Christian prayer.

As emphasized previously, receiving God in one's heart is the most fruitful activity a person can undertake, raising the question: How does a person grow in receptivity? The answer is to cultivate a habit of honestly and consistently acknowledging and relating the affective movements (thoughts, feelings, and desires) of the heart to God. Both honesty and consistency are key.

By honesty, I mean presenting to God our thoughts, feelings, and desires as we find them, coming to Him as we are — not as we wish to be, not as we think we ought to be, not as we hope to be next week or next year or remember being five years ago, not as our parents or our spouse or our buddies want us to be. To be honest is to become aware of and then choose to present to God what is transpiring in our interiority without filter, but with total transparency. This honesty is especially difficult when we fear or despise what we find in our heart, when our thoughts or feelings or desires are messed up. We can take comfort in Jesus who came to seek and save the lost (Lk 19:10), and who reminds us that the healthy do not need a physician, but the sick do (Lk 5:31). If our heart is messed up, who can do anything about it but God? We are not capable of fixing ourselves (or others); we need a savior. So, we can tell Jesus about what we hate in our heart and tell Him that we hate it, and entrust to Him our desire that our heart be transformed, and confess to Him our total poverty in making the change on our own. That is a beautiful way to pray. It gives God great honor and glory. It acknowledges that God is God and we are not.

To grow in intimacy with God, we need to cultivate this honest transparency before God on a consistent basis. This means a daily time of personal prayer each day, but it also means choosing to offer our heart and its movements to God throughout our day. We talk to friends and family all the time about what is happening in our lives and how it affects us. Have we told God first of all? Are we growing in the habit of turning to Him first and with all our heart? Honestly and consistently acknowledging and relating what is in our heart will dispose us to be maximally receptive to God's love. If, for any reason, we do not take the time to be attentive to what is moving in our heart, our intimacy with God will never grow. We will live a very superficial existence, and we will remain a mystery to ourselves. It is astonishing how long we can go in our present culture of distraction without seriously attending to what is transpiring interiorly.

Perhaps I am attentive to the stirrings of my heart but never make the interior leap of entrusting those stirrings to God. I stop at introspection; I acknowledge, but I do not relate. Thus, growth in intimacy is stymied. In truth, our reality is unbearable apart from a vital and intimate relationship with God. For the merely introspective person, introspection will stop, become very superficial, or become unhinged from reality. We all carry brokenness and pain as the sad result of living in a fallen world. The weight of that brokenness and pain is unsustainable and will cause merely introspective persons to stop looking within (or at least not to look too deeply) to seek the relief of distraction, or to escape into fantasy not connected to their interior reality.

Growing in the habit of noticing what is in my heart and telling God all about it invariably disposes my heart to be receptive to God's love. I hear the Gospel at Christmas Mass, and my heart is filled with joy as I sense the tenderness and closeness of Jesus. Do I choose to remain with that particular experience of God's consoling love as I leave Mass, or do I simply go my own way? Do I allow, by choosing to let my heart rest in that felt closeness and tenderness, this particular grace to inspire, direct, and sustain whatever is ahead of me that night, or the next day? It is easy, and a typical temptation, to move away from graces before they achieve the full purpose for which God has given them to us. I am called to allow the love received from God to shape and empower a concrete response. Failure to respond in this organic way to the grace that is offered robs God's love of its life-giving power in my soul. It leaves me adrift, as apart from Him, I can do nothing (Jn 15:5).

At any given moment of prayer or situation in my day, one or another of these dynamics (ARRR) may be more prominent. However, over time, all four must be engaged if my relationship with God is to grow and become more intimate. They need to be engaged when I go to Mass and when I pray the Rosary or Liturgy of the Hours. They need to be engaged in my spiritual reading, my *lectio divina*, and my personal prayer. They need to be engaged as I go to meetings or catch up with my family and my friends. In short, these interior habits need to be cultivated at every moment and in every circumstance of my life. The daily habit of personal prayer is the indispensible spiritual discipline camp to build these habits of interiority.

The Core Curriculum at Work in Scripture: Disciples on the Road to Emmaus

We see these relational dynamics of Acknowledge, Relate, Receive, and Respond many places in Scripture. One example is the disciples on the road to Emmaus (Lk 24:13-35). Cleopas and an unnamed companion are heading seven miles from Jerusalem to Emmaus, "conversing about all the things that had occurred" (Lk 24:14). They are clearly aware of what is on their minds. They *acknowledge* their thoughts, feelings, and desires; and these form the basis of their conversation. Yet, as time goes on, the discussion devolves into a debate (Lk 24:15). The weight of what is transpiring in their hearts is too much; it is burdensome and causes them to be agitated. They talk to each other, but not to God, about what is in their hearts.

Then Jesus draws near them **(Lk 24:15)** and invites them to *relate* what they have been discussing to Him. He asks, "What are you discussing as you walk along?" **(Lk 24:17)** They are resistant, even dismissive: "Are you the only visitor to Jerusalem who does not know ...." **(Lk 24:18)** Jesus is persistent, gentle, and disarming: "What sort of things?" **(Lk 24:19)** We can hear the thoughts, feelings, and desires that accompany the events which the disciples describe **(Lk 24:19-24)**. They are amazed at Jesus, His teaching, and His mighty deeds. They are proud and grateful to have been His disciples. They are saddened at His death and angry and resentful at the chief priests and elders who handed Him over. They are confused and dismayed, even despairing, that the one they thought was the Messiah is now dead, and from such a shameful death. They are astonished at the report of the women who had a vision of angels saying that Jesus is alive. They are wary in their bitter disappointment, and they want to see for themselves. Above all, they, if it is true that Jesus lives, want to see Him. They rushed to the tomb, found everything as the women had said; but Him, they did not see. That is a significant array of deep and complex thoughts, feelings, and desires that comes tumbling out of the disciples. Happily, their *relating* can be messy and imperfect. Intimacy with God does not demand perfect or clinical self-knowledge; it demands honesty and trust. The disciples relate their hearts to Jesus in just this way, and it disposes them to *receive* His consoling love.

"Then beginning with Moses and all the prophets, he interpreted to them what referred to him in all the Scriptures" **(Lk 24:27)**. Their hearts burn within them as He speaks to them **(Lk 24:32)**. This burning is the felt experience of Divine Love (in the form of inspired understanding) touching and transforming their grief, anger, despair, and confusion. Desolation is lifted; consolation takes its place. The disciples have received so much! To put their feelings into perspective, imagine coming back from a holy hour or retreat and, when asked how it went, being able to say, "Oh. God explained everything that referred to Jesus in the Old Testament." Wow! And yet, as the disciples are receiving, a new desire arises in their hearts. They want to receive more. Will they acknowledge and relate this desire to Jesus? Indeed. When it appears that Jesus will leave them, they beg Him to remain **(Lk 24:29)**. And so, they are disposed to receive even more. Jesus remains; and at dinner, He blesses and breaks the bread. Immediately, their eyes are opened, and they recognize Him **(Lk 24:31)**! Their deepest desire is fulfilled.

They have received so much, and these great graces call for a *response*. The disciples do not need a protracted retreat to figure out what to do. Rather, as they are basking in the grace *received*, the *response* is clear. They must return to Jerusalem and tell the others, and they must do so at once **(Lk 24:33)**. Surely, it was work to walk another seven miles back to Jerusalem late at night. But we can readily imagine with what ease and joy those miles slipped by as the disciples were resting in, and being sustained by, the grace they had received.

At Jesus' invitation, the disciples pay attention to what is in their hearts and tell Him all about it. They receive great comfort and consolation as they come to a graced understanding. A new desire arises in their hearts in the midst of receiving this grace, and that desire is entrusted to Jesus; then a greater receiving unfolds at supper. This grace received inspires, directs, and sustains a clear and concrete response in love. Think of how important it was for the Church in its beginning to have Cleopas and the other disciples share their inspired understanding of Scripture. How did their account of recognizing Jesus in the breaking of the bread shed light and understanding on the amazing gift and centrality of the Lord's Supper? How much did their experience bless and shape the Church at its very beginning? How much will our parishes be blessed and shaped according to the loving providence of God as they become genuine schools of prayer and our parishioners learn to receive and respond to God's grace in growing personal intimacy with Him?

BUILDING ON THE FOUNDATION: SUPPLEMENTS TO THE CORE CURRICULUM

Let us take a look at a few special topics that people who are beginning to pray in a relational way encounter:

Silence

Silence is a great help for cultivating the habits of interiority. In our daily lives, we are swept along in a tsunami of noise. Images, music, and information come at us at higher and higher rates, saturating more and more of our environments and activities by way of an ever-expanding array of devices and gadgets. "Be still and know that I am God!" is God's invitation (**Ps 46:11**).

I have the joy and privilege of doing quite a bit of work at Broom Tree, the diocesan retreat center in Sioux Falls, S.D.[33] It is located seven miles west of a town of 396 people. We host silent retreats there. The signature weekend runs from Thursday evening through Sunday afternoon, and it is a silent retreat. There is no cell phone use, no Internet, no magazines or books, apart from Scripture and whatever the spiritual director might suggest for the retreatant. People often arrive at the retreat apprehensive about the silence. They ask themselves, "What will happen if I have no conversation for three full days, if I don't check my messages, my texts, my emails, if I don't do *something*? What will happen if I am still and deeply silent for this period of time?" This type of situation or setting is so different from our daily experience, and people come a little afraid of the silence — but they leave loving it.

Silence amplifies our interior movements. If I am stressed, my stress is amplified in silence. If I am grateful, my gratitude is felt more intensely in silence. If I am confused, I am more fully aware of my confusion in silence. In short, silence helps me experience more directly and distinctly the reality of what is happening within. When this heightened interior awareness is coupled with simple encouragements to honestly relate to God, the retreatants are disposed to receive a whole new lived experience of God's presence, power, and love. And they do.

There is a temptation for the retreatant to attribute these experiences to the place itself. Now, for all its beauty, there is nothing magical about Broom Tree. Three things combine for the powerful and intimate experience of God's love so many receive. These include God's desire for them, their desire for God, and a favorable environment. As the end of the retreat nears, I encourage the participants by saying that God's desire for them is unchanged; it is their desire for God that has grown, and as for the environment, they can make simple choices in daily life to make their home, commute, and even their work more favorable. The first choice on the list, though, is the intentional choice to cultivate silence. Instead of filling the in-between times of the day with television or music or Internet surfing, we can choose silence. We can allow silence to frame, amplify, and clarify the movements of our hearts to more easily relate them honestly to God.

Dealing with Spiritual Desolation

St. Ignatius defines spiritual desolation in the following way: "I call desolation all the contrary of the third rule, such as darkness of soul, disturbance in it, movement to low and earthly things, disquiet from various agitations and temptations, moving to lack of confidence, without hope, without love, finding oneself totally slothful, tepid, sad and, as if separated from one's Creator and Lord. For just as consolation is contrary to desolation, in the same way the thoughts that come from consolation are contrary to the thoughts that come from desolation."[34]

The trial of spiritual desolation is the main stumbling block that hinders a person from being consistent in cultivating a deeper intimacy with the Father, Son, and Holy Spirit in prayer. While a full treatment of discernment of spirits is beyond the scope of this book,[35] a few essentials must be mentioned.

Spiritual consolation and desolation are experienced as thoughts, feelings, and desires in the heart. What distinguishes these interior movements from other, non-spiritual, movements is that they impact directly on one's relationship with God and carrying out His will. I can watch a beautiful sunset and feel peaceful and relaxed. This is not spiritual consolation; it is non-spiritual consolation. But, perhaps, as I am watching the sunset, my heart is moved with amazement at God's creativity; and I have a heightened awareness of how beautiful God must be as the Creator of the sunset. That amazement (feeling) and awareness (thought) are spiritual in nature. They are spiritual consolation. The disturbance, disquiet, agitation, temptation, lack of confidence, slothfulness, tepidity, sadness, and felt separation Ignatius speaks of in the aforementioned quote have as their focus my relationship with God and carrying out His will. They are *spiritual* desolation.

God always labors to console us. God never makes us desolate, and spiritual desolation always is to be resisted. How? The aim of spiritual desolation is to get us to turn in upon ourselves and stop relating to God. One way to resist desolation is to simply acknowledge it and relate it honestly to God, and to ask for what we want, namely, to be delivered from the trial of desolation. In his letter to the Philippians, St. Paul gives excellent and practical counsel in this regard:

Rejoice in the Lord always. I shall say it again: rejoice! Your kindness should be known to all. The Lord is near. Have no anxiety at all, but in everything, by prayer and petition, with thanksgiving, make your requests known to God. Then the peace of God that surpasses all understanding will guard your hearts and minds in Christ Jesus. Finally, brothers, whatever is true, whatever is honorable, whatever is just, whatever is pure, whatever is lovely, whatever is gracious, if there is any excellence and if there is anything worthy of praise, think about these things. Keep on doing what you have learned and received and heard and seen in me. Then the God of peace will be with you (Phil 4:4-9).

St. Paul calls us to rejoice *in the Lord*, to receive the gift of Jesus, who is the cause of our joy, and to do so always. Is this possible? Is this just pie-in-the-sky Pollyanna-ism? This is the same St. Paul who suffered greatly — physically, emotionally, and spiritually — in his apostolic ministry.[36] The truth of the Lord's closeness is the foundation of our rejoicing always. When anxiety threatens the joy and peace of Christ in our hearts, what shall we do? By prayer and petition, together with thanksgiving, we are to make our requests known to God. "Prayer," here, means telling God all about it. The petition is asking God for what we desire, entrusting our desire to God by making our requests known to Him. And we are to pray and make petition together with thanksgiving.

This prayer of thanksgiving to God in the midst of suffering is not easy. In the trial of desolation, the last thing on earth I want to do is talk to God about what is going on in my heart. First of all, what is in my heart is painful and difficult. I would much rather not pay attention to it at all. I would rather lose myself in some entertainment or "productive" endeavor that does not demand interior awareness. Secondly, in desolation, it feels as though God is far away, that I am separated from Him. Discouragement fills my heart. "What good will it do to talk to God?" I say to myself. It can seem like an insurmountable obstacle to make the effort to attend to what is in my heart and to tell God about it.

It is at this point in our thinking where thanksgiving comes in. St. Paul directs us to think about — to fix our attention on — what is true, honorable, just, pure, lovely, gracious, to look around at our situation to see if there is any excellence or anything worthy of praise. This advice is not about the "the power of positive thinking." It is not a pop psychology device to "look on the bright side" or adopt an optimistic outlook. It is an invitation to notice the presence of God. He is true, lovely, gracious, etc., and is all those things without limit. Every experience I have of these qualities is a reflection of God's presence, love, and goodness. St. Paul is inviting us to notice the dandelions, so to speak, just as the mom in the aforementioned example did when her son gave them to her. St. Paul wants us to receive the concrete expressions of God's love in our lived experience. When love is received in the heart, gratitude naturally arises. This gratitude is like an engine in our hearts (think "The Little Engine That Could"), which gives us the energy necessary to look with courage on the desolating movements of our hearts and to entrust them to God. What is the result of following this counsel? Spiritual consolation returns. The God of peace is with us, His peace guarding our hearts and minds in Christ Jesus.

Dealing with Distraction

Anyone who has made a genuine attempt to cultivate a consistent habit of prayer has encountered the difficulty of distraction. Sometimes a distraction is just a distraction. At other times, distraction reveals an attachment in the heart that needs to be transformed by Divine Love. "To set about hunting down distractions would be to fall into their trap, when all that is necessary is to turn back to our heart: for a distraction reveals to us what we are attached to, and this humble awareness before the Lord should awaken our preferential love for him and lead us resolutely to offer him our heart to be purified."[37]

Following is a simple three-step process for dealing with distraction in prayer. It is based on having a *simple* plan for prayer before sitting down to pray. For now, consider a plan to meditate on the Baptism of the Lord during your holy hour. You can begin by reading through the passage in the Gospel of Mark that describes Jesus' Baptism and trying to imagine the scene. Ten minutes go by, and you realize that you have not been attending to the passage at all, but have been thinking instead about a letter you have to write for an upcoming deanery meeting. The first step, once you realize you are distracted, is to *very gently* return to whatever you had planned to pay attention to. Thus, go back very gently to the passage, and begin to read it through again. The gentleness is key, lest in your frustration or self-recrimination, you subtly set about hunting down the cause of the distraction and, thereby, fall into its trap.

Some more moments pass, and once again, you find yourself distracted. This time, it is not the letter, but rather, thinking about a number of phone calls you need to return. You notice that this distraction is in the same "box" as your first distraction. It is "stuff" you have to get done and could be doing now instead of taking this time to pray. When you are distracted again by the same thing or something like it, you move to step two and tell God all about the distraction: "God, I want to be with Jesus at His Baptism; I want to hear You say to my heart that I am Your beloved son. I am distracted by this letter that has to go out today, and these phone calls. I had planned to do them this morning, but was called to the hospital. Grrr. I'm annoyed that I keep thinking about these things instead of being with Jesus. I know You will provide the time I need to take care of the rest of that stuff. Help me to trust You. Father, help me to be with Jesus in His Baptism."

Having told God about the distraction and asked for what your heart desires, you should *very gently* return to the passage and begin again to meditate on Christ's Baptism.

The third time the same or a closely related distraction comes along, it is time to scrap your plan for prayer and pray instead with the distraction. A real distraction will never survive step two. If it comes back a third time, it is not a distraction, but rather, something God sees in your heart that He wants you to give to Him. So, pay attention to the substance of the distraction. Relate honestly to God the thoughts, feelings, and desires that accompany it, and see what unfolds.

Finally, it is possible that you spend your hour distracted by a series of completely unrelated things. In my experience, this is rare; but it is possible. In this case, you need to continue repeating step one. If you spend your whole hour of prayer doing this, it will not be very enjoyable, but it certainly will be fruitful. Returning our attention to God is always fruitful.

Is This Real or Am I Making It Up?

If parishioners take up the invitation to begin a daily habit of prayer, they will very quickly begin to have a whole new lived experience of the presence, power, and love of God. Yet, they will still experience the reality of their sin. In fact, in the light of God's love, they may well be even more aware of their sin. This tension, along with the dynamics of spiritual desolation, can make the person question whether their grace-filled and consoling experiences in prayer are real or just made up.

To address this common concern, we can look at the difference between Christian imagination and fantasy. Fantasy has no foundation in reality. If I am watching *The Shining*, the movie will have an effect on me. I will get scared. If something happens suddenly, I may even jump in my seat or cry out. But the effect has no grounding in reality. As soon as I stop engaging the fantasy, the movie ends, and the lights come on; the effect of the fantasy evaporates. Not so with Christian imagination.

Christian imagination seizes on spiritual *reality* and translates it into something that literally makes sense to me, something that I can see, hear, taste, touch, and smell. "Taste and see that the Lord is good" **(Ps 34:9)**. How is this possible? God is an infinite and eternal spirit. He does not register in my physical senses. My five physical senses have counterparts — the spiritual senses. Physical senses have as their proper object physical reality. Sight is attuned to light; smell, to odor; taste, to flavor; touch, to texture; and hearing, to sound. The spiritual senses are attuned to spiritual reality — God, the Father, Son, and Holy Spirit, angels and demons, and human souls. They seize on spiritual reality and translate it in such a way that the spiritual dimension becomes sensible. The information gathered by the spiritual senses is summed up in Christian imagination.

Like fantasy, spiritual *reality* has an effect on me. As I pray with the account of Peter walking on the water and engage my spiritual senses, imagining the feel of the water, the sound of the storm, the rocking of the boat, the appearance of Jesus, etc., I find myself in Peter's place at the moment he is sinking and cries out, "Lord, save me!" *Immediately*, Jesus took him by the hand. What arrests my attention is the word "immediately." As I stay with this word, a *sense* of Jesus' strength and a sense of total security and confidence fill my heart. Am I making this sense up, or is it real? Unlike fantasy, the effect that spiritual realities have on us continues after we are no longer actively engaged in the meditation or contemplation. As I go about my day, and I simply glance interiorly at that moment in my prayer, as I go back to that word "immediately," is the awareness of Jesus' strength and my own security and confidence in Him still active? It is, and this is a clear indication that I did not just make up that experience in my prayer.

Finally, since our spiritual senses engage spiritual reality, the exercise of Christian imagination always draws my attention to God — His presence, His power, His love, and His activity. If I, or someone or something else, start taking the center place of my attention in prayer, it is a good sign that I have jumped from meditation on reality into fantasy. And fantasy masquerading as prayer always will leave the person spiritually desolate. The Father, Son, and Holy Spirit always are the most real persons in the room, at every moment, at every place, and in every circumstance in human history. Period. Not to be in touch with this reality is to be out of touch with reality. We do well to cultivate the use of our spiritual senses so we can overcome our habitual insanity of living as if God is not. Fantasy, then, is images disconnected from reality. And what is imagination? It is the work of affectively filled images connecting to the truth of the Paschal Mystery of Christ. If we want our minds to stay connected to reality, then we have to have the images in our minds stay connected to the source of all reality itself, the Truth Himself — Christ.

How Do I Know I Am Praying Correctly?

Related to the fear that we are just making up consoling experiences in prayer is the insecurity and second-guessing that happens in a time of spiritual desolation. People undergoing the trial of desolation often will wonder about their prayer: "Am I doing this right? It seems something is going wrong." The alternation of spiritual consolation and desolation is expected. It is a natural ebb-and-flow in the spiritual life. We are called to a specific spiritual response in each case, namely, to receive spiritual consolation and to resist spiritual desolation with the help of God's grace. So, when a person begins to doubt if he is praying "rightly," here are two simple measures: honesty and consistency. In my prayer and throughout my day, am I coming to God as I am, transparently, *honestly* entrusting to Him the thoughts, feelings, and desires that are in my heart? Am I taking time each day, *consistently*, in personal prayer to do so? If the answer to both of these questions is "Yes," I can rest assured that my relationship with God is growing and will continue to be fruitful, although I do not feel that this is true at all in the midst of desolation. The enemy's aim in making us desolate is ultimately to have us give up taking the steps that will lead us to deeper intimacy with God. Often, the path to such discouragement is by way of a wild goose chase trying to "fix" our prayer when, in fact, nothing is wrong with it. Such a quixotic quest can deplete our spiritual energies for pursuing God in prayer, frequent reception of the Sacraments, and a daily diet of Scripture, service, and good fellowship. The honesty/ consistency review can help us defeat the temptations of Satan.

chapter 3

Classrooms for the School of Prayer

The Mystical Nativity by Sandro Botticelli

Acknowledge, Relate, Receive, and Respond (ARRR) form the core curriculum of the school of prayer. In addition to a curriculum, a school needs a place for the teaching to happen. What are the classrooms of the parish's school of prayer?

THE MASS

The Mass is the great prayer of the Church. "The Eucharist contains and expresses all forms of prayer: it is 'the pure offering' of the whole Body of Christ to the glory of God's name…."[38] Though everyone processes up to the altar to receive the Precious Body and the Precious Blood, how many really receive Communion with Christ in a deepening personal intimacy? The Mass is the first and inexhaustible venue to teach prayer and to assist people to allow their hearts to be caught up into the great and perfect prayer of Christ.

Acknowledging, relating, receiving, and responding comprise the entire Mass. From the very beginning of the Mass, we acknowledge the Trinity's presence: "In the Name of the Father, and of the Son, and of the Holy Spirit. The Lord be with you. And with your spirit." Next, we acknowledge and relate our need for mercy: "I confess to almighty God and to you, my brothers and sisters." We receive God's living Word in Scripture. We respond in the responsorial psalm. And so on and so forth throughout the Mass. The priest can easily teach his people to pay attention to these relational dynamics in the Mass and to encourage his people to enter into them personally. Doing so helps the parishioners experience the Mass as more than just going through the motions and can powerfully awaken their desire to grow in personal relationship with God. At the penitential rite, the priest can encourage them to really acknowledge and relate the particular ways they are in need of God's forgiveness and mercy, so that the Confiteor becomes a real and beautiful public confession and the Kyrie a personal plea. At the offertory, people can be easily taught to make a real offering of their hearts, their situations, their cares and concerns, as true gifts, the good the bad and the ugly, upon the altar so that by Christ's sacrifice and the outpouring of the Holy Spirit, they may be redeemed, transfigured, and sanctified. At the preparation for Communion: "… but only say the word and my soul shall be healed," the priest can lead his people in expectant faith, teaching them to exercise and entrust to God their personal and particular needs to be healed and set free. In the time after Communion, he can lead them to notice the particular way God is loving them. Spiritual consolation (the particular consoling thought, feeling, desire) is union with God in the way God is making it possible for the individual to receive.

These ways of being at Mass constitute full, active, and conscious participation in it. The priest can greatly assist his people in such participation by being generous with liturgical silence. Silence is a great and rare treasure in the world, and the Liturgy calls for it. The priest can offer this silence, especially after the homily and after Communion. Several minutes of silence! While it will take a little getting used to, if the priest will teach his people what to do with the silence (to acknowledge what stirs in their hearts, to relate these movements to God with trust and honesty, to rest and receive any particular felt experience of God's love, presence, power, to listen for the voice of God inspiring a personal response), the great prayer of the Mass will become more and more a prayerful and transforming encounter with the living God.

Some may object that Mass will go too long if we take a couple *minutes* of silence after the homily and Communion. There is a simple and needed solution: Preach shorter homilies, and preach differently.[39] As a mode of communicating information, the homily is inefficient. Honestly, how much of the homily from

Sunday does a typical parishioner remember by Thursday — or even by the time he leaves the parking lot? On the other hand, the homily can be a very effective means of disposing the hearts of the parishioners to encounter God in a deep and intimate way. If the priest allows the homily to be a public contemplation, a gazing with love on the mystery and reality of God revealed in the Scripture, he can draw their attention, not to himself, his theological knowledge, or his anecdotal information, but to God, to the Mystery. The aim of the homily should be to gather the people together and lead them to the Bridegroom and then leave them with Jesus to behold and be beheld. The generous silence after the homily reverences this unique intimacy of Christ with each person present, an intimacy to which the priest, by his contemplative preaching, has issued an invitation and pointed the way. The closeness with Jesus uniquely experienced in each heart will never be forgotten and will bear abundant fruit.

CONFESSION

Confession is another privileged classroom for the school of prayer. It is a unique opportunity to teach people the importance of growing relational attentiveness to the stirrings of their hearts. Any Catholic who has made a regular habit of going to confession has experienced the frustration and discouragement of the "laundry list," those habitual and recurring sins they just cannot seem to get past. Indeed, many Catholics have stopped going to confession altogether because they have drawn the conclusion that "nothing seems to change; it doesn't do me any good." When the priest confessor detects that kind of frustration and discouragement in a penitent, he has the opportunity to teach the penitent the value of Acknowledge, Relate, Receive, and Respond. Has the penitent told God about his frustration and discouragement? What happens if he does? Can the penitent name what was going on in his heart at the time of the temptation, the hour, the day, the week before the temptation? Sometimes the penitent cannot. Often he can. This knowledge of the heart's movements opens the way for profound healing and conversion.

In reality, we are not randomly tempted. Instead, the evil spirit attacks us at our weakest point.[40] God made us to be loved by others as He loves us, with a free, total, faithful, and life-giving love. Whenever we are treated in an un-loving way, damage is done; our hearts are wounded. Sometimes, it is just a scratch or a paper cut; sometimes, it is an amputation. In any case, with the wound, naturally, comes pain and fear. Unless the love of God enters that wound, healing the damage caused by the absence of love, we are vulnerable to spiritual attack. Spiritual desolation is the first wave of the attack. Desolation lives in and feeds off of wounds like an opportunistic infection. If spiritual desolation is not resisted, it will crystallize into temptation, which puts forth an empty promise to relieve, not heal, our pain. If temptation is not resisted, we will sin, which, in turn, does more damage (this time, self-inflicted) to the heart; and a vicious cycle unfolds.

The priest can teach and assist the penitent in naming the spiritually desolating thoughts, feelings, and desires that accompany temptation and lead the penitent to honestly relate them to God. As the penitent makes the graced decision to do so, and invites God to come into those thoughts, feelings, and desires with His love, real healing and conversion unfold. The merciful love of God always is aimed at the root of sin, so once it is received, sin will not grow back. The poverty of our sinfulness is a particular and motivating occasion to learn and practice relational prayer so we might enjoy a deep and intimate experience of the healing power of God's mercy in the Sacrament of Reconciliation.

COMMITTEE MEETINGS

In a busy parish, the priest will spend a lot of time in meetings of various sorts. What would happen if the "business" of the parish were addressed in an environment of encounter with God, instead of one of just trying to figure out what to do? The priest forming his parish as a school of prayer can take advantage of his committee meetings to do so. Instead of a more or less perfunctory opening prayer, what if the members of the parish staff (or pastoral or finance council) were led in 15 minutes of *lectio divina* with the Gospel of the day, followed by a sharing of graces received? What if, in the midst of deliberations, the priest led the group in a "pause of the spirit?" For example, he could lead the group in a decade of the Rosary, inviting them to entrust their ideas and desires regarding the matter at hand to God, and asking to be able to receive His Holy Spirit's Inspiration with docility. Following the pause, there can be a kind of heart-sharing with members describing what transpired for them during the moment of recollection. Priests will be amazed and delighted with what a difference this makes in attending to parish business, organizing activities, planning, etc. Christ is real. He is present; He is acting. The question to ask Jesus in our parish meetings is, "Jesus, what are *You* doing?" so that we can choose to remain with Him, because apart from Him, *we* can do nothing. The priest has a great opportunity in his different meetings to teach the essential habits of interiority to his parishioners.

THE HOME

The parish is a family of families. The ultimate aim of forming the parish as a school of prayer is to foster "homeschooling." A child should learn the habits of interiority from his mom and dad.[41] Of course, parents cannot give what they have not received.

In marriage preparation, RCIA, and other adult faith formation opportunities, and above all, in his coming to know and befriend families in the parish, the priest has a great opportunity to teach teachers how to teach prayer. He can begin by helping husbands and wives to learn how to pray together as a couple.[42] This step is predicated on each of them first growing in the habit of their own personal prayer.

When I come to know a husband and wife and know that both of them are beginning to cultivate the habit of daily personal relational prayer, I propose to them a daily intentional conversation with each other. This conversation has some very important ground rules: 1) it is not a time to "work on the relationship"; 2) it is not a time to arrange the carpools for the kids or to organize other domestic details; 3) it is not a time to offer advice, to problem-solve, or to try to figure out or fix anything; and 4) it is not a time to talk about others, unless the purpose of that talking is to reveal how another's actions or words affected the husband or wife. All these things are fine in themselves, just not during this conversation. This conversation is a time for the spouses to reveal to each other what has been on their hearts and minds that day. It is a time for them to entrust their thoughts and feelings and desires to each other and to experience their spouse listening to them and receiving them with unconditional love.

The inclination to offer advice or to try to fix some difficulty for one's spouse must be stubbornly resisted. If we are honest with ourselves, we know we really are powerless to fix things for others anyway. When we love another, it is painful to see that person burdened or troubled in any way. It is natural to want to jump in and "make it better." But here we are confronted with our essential poverty. God alone is the one who can really heal, and lift burdens, and create new realities in us and around us and among us.

I propose to praying couples that they take 30 minutes for this intentional conversation. Whoever goes first is simply and honestly sharing what has been on his heart and mind that day. The other is attentively listening and striving to receive his spouse's self-revelation with unconditional love. The one who has been listening then takes what he has heard and offers a prayer to — God — out loud. He relates to God what he has heard and what he desires for his spouse as he has listened. An example of the listening spouse's prayer might be as follows: "Heavenly Father, you know the sadness Jenny has in her heart over Dad's death, and she thinks she should be over it by now. You know how much he meant to her, and the worry she has for her mom now. I thank you, Father, for her beautiful heart and ask you to come into her sorrow and worry and to bless her with your love. Amen."

The prayer is a very simple matter of the listening spouse offering to God whatever stirs in his heart as he has been listening. He has welcomed his spouse and all that the spouse has shared into his heart; and now, they both lift their hearts up to God in prayer. In doing so, the spouse who has been sharing will experience being listened to attentively by her beloved, being received with love by her beloved, and will be the witness to the beauty of her beloved lifting her and her experiences up to God and interceding for her. Then, it is time to switch roles. This conversation is very intimate, very vulnerable (and, therefore, threatening), but also surpassingly beautiful and healing for the couple. It can open up a depth of union and love for the couple far beyond anything they can ask for or imagine.

Couples who take up this invitation discover that their children tend to be drawn to them whenever they begin this conversation. It is great for children to know that Mom and Dad love them, but what a child wants most is to be safe, immersed, and welcomed into the communion of love that gave rise to his life in the first place. So, the children may want to be with the parents. And that is OK, as long as they are not diverting the attention of Mom and Dad away from each other. They can be in the room, but should be occupied by their own pursuits and not in a position to interrupt Mom and Dad's intimate time.

A couple who takes up this adventure of really sharing their hearts with each other and praying together will have ample opportunity to cultivate a similar intimacy with their children. They will learn the essential habits of *unlocking* their children's hearts. I often ask parents how many conversations with their children really reveal what is happening in their children's hearts. When their hearts are revealed, how many of those revelations are met with unconditional love and shared prayer instead of advice or correction? The answer is "not many." Of course, parents need to teach, advise, and discipline their children. But if Mom and Dad learn the habit of praying together, each of them alone and both of them together can find regular opportunities to bless their children by inviting their children's self revelation. The children can experience the unique gift of being listened to attentively, received unconditionally, and lifted up to God by parents who love them. This self revelation cultivates an intimacy and trust in love that will make it possible for children to receive and even to seek out their parents' advice and correction when it counts.[43]

Parish Religious Education

The priest who strives to form his parish as a school of prayer will naturally have opportunities to teach prayer in the various venues of religious education with which he is involved. I leave this classroom to the last because didactic teaching of prayer is, perhaps, the least effective. There are a myriad of books available on prayer, which are bought and presumably read; but how many people are really praying in a consistent and relational way? My simple encouragement here is that the best way to teach prayer is to present a few basics such as Acknowledge, Relate, Receive, and

Respond (ARRR). Simply. Briefly. Then, actually lead people in the experience of prayer. The lab practicum is far more effective than the textbook. So, even in a classroom setting, across a wide array of ages, the priest can invite people to pay attention to, for example, a passage of Scripture. Then, he can lead them to notice what stirs in their hearts, to acknowledge and relate honestly to God the thoughts, feelings, and desires that are present in them. That will dispose their hearts to receive from God. At the end, he can invite a simple "sharing of graces," asking those involved to share something of their experience. Doing so is a good and effective way to introduce people to the idea of relational prayer itself.

More fruitful still is for the priest to adopt a contemplative methodology in all the teaching he does, which includes coaching students to contemplatively receive the material presented.[44] He should encourage students to notice what arrests their attention and the affective movements that accompany their attention being arrested. He should teach them the habit of noting for themselves these affective responses alongside, but separate from, their usual informational notes. He should teach them the habit of asking essential questions, such as: What is being said (didactic information)? How does this information speak to me? What does this information lead me to want to say to God? What is God saying to me in this information? The priest should provide opportunities in class to pause, be in silence, and enter into prayer, always helping the class know what to do in the silence. In doing so, he is teaching his students that the heart can be engaged in receiving the faith. Allowing time for that process to occur overcomes the danger of the faith being experienced merely as an abstract set of ideas. Teaching in a contemplative fashion and helping students to learn in a contemplative fashion can awaken the students' *desire* to know more and unleash their willingness to expend the energy necessary to acquire greater knowledge.

chapter 4

Simple Plans
for Prayer

Supper at Emmaus by Rembrandt Harmenszoon van Rijn

I have identified four essential dynamics (ARRR) or interior habits for growing in relational prayer and intimacy with the Father, Son, and Holy Spirit. These dynamics should be present in any form or method of Christian prayer, if the prayer is to be fruitful and result in growing Trinitarian intimacy. To form the parish as a school of prayer, the priest must consistently form and encourage the practice of Scripture study to include the steps of acknowledging, relating, receiving, and responding though, in and of themselves, they are not a method of prayer. For people who are beginning to take a daily time for personal prayer, it is often helpful to suggest one or another form or method of prayer in which these interior habits can be practiced. Many books and articles can offer such suggestions.[45] I offer here a simple format for a daily period of prayer.

Preparation

Before the time of prayer arrives, the person should decide a few simple things:

1) *Where will I go to pray?*
The chapel? My bedroom? The park bench?

2) *At what time and for how long will I pray?*
There is no magical amount of time that is best, but I find that, at a minimum, people need 30 minutes, mostly because, in a busy day, it can take 10 or 15 minutes just for the cacophony of thoughts, feelings, and desires to quiet down enough for one to notice what is really going on inside oneself. It is important to stick with the pre-determined length of prayer, whether it is full of consolation, arid, or just very ordinary.

3) *What do I want to pay attention to or pray with?*
Perhaps one wants to use a passage from Scripture, a chapter of a

good spiritual book, the Joyful Mysteries of the Rosary, or just a single decade of the Rosary. Maybe one wants to talk to God about what is going on with one's boss or spouse, or one wants to sing praise and worship songs to God. These are all great options. The key is to pick something specific to pay attention to as you begin to pray.

4) *What grace do I want to ask of God?*

This grace should be personal and specific. This is not an intercession for others or for the world. The grace one asks is a specific desire for some good gift he or she wants from God to help them in their relationship with Him and carrying out His will. Examples of what to ask are as follows: "Father, help me to have a whole new lived experience of Your infinite and personal love for me." "Jesus, free me from the discouragement that is filling my heart."

AS THE TIME FOR PRAYER ARRIVES

1) *Call to mind the presence of God.*

St. Ignatius, speaking of his own life, suggests that at the beginning of each period of prayer, "I will stand for the space of an Our Father, a step or two before the place where I am to meditate or contemplate, and with my mind raised on high, consider that God our Lord beholds me…."[46] The point here is that prayer is a relational encounter with God, Who is present and loving us at every moment. We want to let our hearts register the reality of God's presence so that our prayers are a response to Him, instead of an insecure throwing out of words and sentiments on the off chance He might be around. Incidentally, whenever one feels "stuck" during a period of prayer, coming back to focus on the reality of God's presence, at that very moment, is very helpful. Sometimes this awareness comes together imaginatively as an image of being with the Father, or Jesus, or the Holy Spirit, in a particular place.

2) Begin with the Sign of the Cross and invocation of the Holy Spirit.

The Holy Spirit is the master of prayer. We want to invoke his assistance as we begin to pray.

3) Ask for the grace you desire.

To ask for the grace is exercising the desire and entrusting that desire to God.

4) Turn your attention to whatever desire or thought with which you decided to pray.

5) When the heart is stirred or engaged, acknowledge and relate those thoughts, feelings, and desires.

If you experience spiritual consolation, rest in it and receive it. Do not be in a rush to get back to the passage or Rosary, etc.

6) When the stirring of the heart subsides and has run its course, return to the passage, or Rosary or whatever you are praying with until the heart is moved again.

7) If nothing seems to be happening, tell God all about the "nothing."

Am I bored, angry, etc.? What do I want?

8) At the end of the period, pray a colloquy:

The colloquy is a beautiful three to five minutes of conversation with the Trinity or Saints at the end of the period of prayer. Imagine yourself with Jesus. However that comes together is fine. As you sense yourself with Jesus, look into your heart, and offer Him whatever you find. This might be a request, a complaint, a question, a word of thanks or praise, a song, a verse from Scripture, or a memory. Whatever it is, offer it to Jesus. Then repeat this process with the Father, and then again, with the Holy Spirit. Imagine yourself with Them. Look into your heart, and offer whatever you find. This regular practice of the colloquy heightens the experience of intimacy with the Father, Son, and Holy Spirit. The colloquy is a natural and relational way to conclude the time of prayer, instead of just stopping.

REVIEW OF PRAYER

After the prayer, take a break for a few minutes, and then journal for yourself brief and simple answers to these questions: What was I feeling? What did I desire? What was I thinking? What did I receive from God?

The goal here is not to record every thought, feeling, and desire, but to look back over the whole period of prayer and simply note what stands out to you. It can be accomplished with a couple of sentences. This frees you as you are praying to simply note what stirs in your heart, instead of analyzing it, judging it, or trying to be sure to remember it. If you start doing so during the prayer, the movement of the heart will be interrupted. With the help of the regular review of prayer, you can begin to see the organic movement of God's grace in your heart, what He is saying, what He is touching and healing, and what He is asking of you in response. You will more readily identify areas of resistance in your heart where you begin to pull away from God in prayer.

CONCLUSION

The dignity of man rests, above all, on the fact that he is called to communion with God. The invitation to converse with God is addressed to man as soon as he comes into being. For if man exists, it is because God has created him through love, and through love, continues to hold him in existence. He cannot live fully according to truth unless he freely acknowledges that love and entrusts himself to his Creator.[47]

It should never be forgotten that prayer constitutes an essential part of Christian life, understood in its fullness and centrality. Indeed, prayer is an important part of our very humanity: it is "the first expression of man's inner truth, the first condition for authentic freedom of spirit."[48]

Far from being a form of escapism from everyday commitments, prayer constitutes the strongest incentive for the Christian family to assume and comply fully with all its responsibilities as the primary and fundamental cell of human society. Thus, the Christian family's actual participation in the Church's life and mission is in direct proportion to the fidelity and intensity of the prayer with which it is united with the fruitful vine that is Christ the Lord.

The fruitfulness of the Christian family in its specific service to human advancement, which, of itself, cannot but lead to the transformation of the world, derives from its living union with Christ, nourished by Liturgy, by self-oblation and by prayer.[49]

We know well, in fact, that prayer cannot be taken for granted. We must learn how to pray, almost as if acquiring this art anew; even those who are very advanced in the spiritual life always feel the need to enter the school of Jesus to learn to pray with authenticity[50]

I have endeavored to present Christ's call through the Church for priests to form their parishes as schools of prayer. I have proposed a "core curriculum" for the school of prayer, and suggested various favorable settings in the parish for this formation to take place. More needs to be said on all of these topics, but I hope these reflections offer a helpful starting point and encouragement to my brother priests. God calls us to intimacy with Himself, so we might love our people more, and serve them as master teachers of prayer, that they may live fully their vocations and take up their irreplaceable roles in the New Evangelization for the transformation of the world in Christ.

Endnotes

1   Blessed John Paul II, Apostolic Letter *Novo Millennio Ineunte*, nos. 32-33, Jan. 6, 2001.

2   "Today, having a clear faith based on the Creed of the Church is often labeled as fundamentalism. Whereas relativism, that is, letting oneself be 'tossed here and there, carried about by every wind of doctrine', seems the only attitude that can cope with modern times. We are building a dictatorship of relativism that does not recognize anything as definitive and whose ultimate goal consists solely of one's own ego and desires.

"We, however, have a different goal: the Son of God, the true man. He is the measure of true humanism. An 'adult' faith is not a faith that follows the trends of fashion and the latest novelty; a mature adult faith is deeply rooted in friendship with Christ. It is this friendship that opens us up to all that is good and gives us a criterion by which to distinguish the true from the false, and deceit from truth.

"We must develop this adult faith; we must guide the flock of Christ to this faith. And it is this faith - only faith - that creates unity and is fulfilled in love." Joseph Cardinal Ratzinger, *Homily at Mass for the Election of the Supreme Pontiff*, St. Peter's Basilica, 18 April 2005.

3   "We live in a culture of distraction — addiction to technological entertainment, impatience with all manner of suffering or limit, a thirst for immediacy, an obsession with lust, a craving for speed, a decadent voracity for food. In receiving this culture within our minds and affect we receive only anxiety. Due to our sophistication in technology we have more leisure but, unfortunately, no rest. Why? Simply put, when the culture of distraction defines us we become more filled with the self, the ego. Everything becomes measured on the scale of usefulness to and entertainment for *the self*. Intrinsic value is jettisoned for utilitarian value." Deacon James Keating, Ph.D., "The Parish as a School of Prayer," *Emmanuel* (July/Aug. 2008): 306.

4   St. Augustine, Confessions, Book 1, Chapter1.

5   Blessed John Paul II, *Novo Millennio Ineunte*, no. 33.

6   Ibid.

7   Blessed John Paul II, *Address to the Austrian Bishops, June 21, 1998*

8   Pope Benedict XVI, *Address By the Holy Father Meeting With The Clergy*, Warsaw Cathedral, May 25, 2006.

9   Blessed John Paul II, *Pastores Dabo Vobis*, no.45.

10   "Ordained ministers are also responsible for the formation in prayer of their brothers and sisters in Christ. Servants of the Good Shepherd, they are ordained to lead the People of God to the living waters of prayer: the Word of God, the liturgy, the theological life (the life of faith, hope, and charity), and the Today of God in concrete situations." *Catechism of the Catholic Church*, no. 2686.

11   Pope Benedict XVI, *Address By the Holy Father Meeting With The Clergy.*

[12] Ibid.

[13] Cf. *Catechism of the Catholic Church*, nos. 2725-2745.

[14] "The Father and I are one." Jn 10:30.

[15] "Amen, amen, I say to you, a son cannot do anything on his own, but only what he sees his father doing; for what he does, his son will do also. For the Father loves his Son and shows him everything that he himself does, and he will show him greater works than these, so that you may be amazed." Jn 5:19-20. Similarly, "…I do nothing on my own, but I say only what the Father taught me. The one who sent me is with me." Jn 8:28-29.

[16] *Catechism of the Catholic Church*, no. 2601.

[17] Keating, "The Parish as a School of Prayer," p. 308.

[18] *Catechism of the Catholic Church*, no. 2567.

[19] "The most common yet most hidden temptation is our *lack of faith*. It expresses itself less by declared incredulity than by our actual preferences. When we begin to pray, a thousand labors or cares thought to be urgent vie for priority; once again, it is the moment of truth for the heart: what is its real love? Sometimes we turn to the Lord as a last resort, but do we really believe he is? Sometimes we enlist the Lord as an ally, but our heart remains presumptuous. In each case, our lack of faith reveals that we do not yet share in the disposition of a humble heart: 'without me, you can do *nothing*.'" *Catechism of the Catholic Church*, no. 2732. Cf. Jn 15:5.

[20] Pope Benedict XVI, *Address by the Holy Father Meeting with the Clergy,* Warsaw Cathedral, May 25, 2006.

[21] Pope Benedict XVI, *Address to Priests and Permanent Deacons*, (prepared text), Freising Cathedral, Sept. 14, 2006.

[22] "But we who have received the grace of believing in Christ, the revealer of the Father and the Saviour of the world, have a duty to show to what depths the relationship with Christ can lead.

"The great mystical tradition of the Church of both East and West has much to say in this regard. It shows how prayer can progress, as a genuine dialogue of love, to the point of rendering the person wholly possessed by the divine Beloved, vibrating at the Spirit's touch, resting filially within the Father's heart. This is the lived experience of Christ's promise: 'He who loves me will be loved by my Father, and I will love him and manifest myself to him' (*Jn* 14:21). It is a journey totally sustained by grace, which nonetheless demands an intense spiritual commitment and is no stranger to painful purifications (the 'dark night'). But it leads, in various possible ways, to the ineffable joy experienced by the mystics as 'nuptial union.'" Blessed John Paul II, *Novo Millenio Ineunte*, no. 33.

23 "The heart is the dwelling-place where I am, where I live; according to the Semitic or Biblical expression, the heart is the place 'to which I withdraw.' The heart is our hidden center, beyond the grasp of our reason and of others; only the Spirit of God can fathom the human heart and know it fully. The heart is the place of decision, deeper than our psychic drives. It is the place of truth, where we choose life or death. It is the place of encounter, because as image of God we live in relation: it is the place of covenant." *Catechism of the Catholic Church*, no. 2563.

24 "Goods of the senses are more visible, more tangible, and more readily apparent to us than those of the mind and of the spiritual order. Consequently we are easily drawn 'without,' toward what our senses can grasp, while greater effort is required to attend to the less perceptible world 'within.'…Electronic means of filling the quiet spaces continue to multiply: portable TV's, cell phones, the Internet, and the like. A secularized worldview questions faith and the reality itself of an interior spiritual life. Accordingly, the value of noticing different spiritual voices in our hearts is simply unrecognized." Father Timothy Gallagher, *The Discernment of Spirits: An Ignatian Guide for Everyday Living* (New York: Crossroad Publishing Company, 2005), p. 19.

25 For a discussion of what realities are encompassed by the terms "good spirit" and "evil spirit," see Gallagher, *Discernment*, pp. 32-37.

26 "Christian prayer…flees from impersonal techniques or from concentrating on oneself, which can create a kind of rut, imprisoning the person praying in a spiritual privatism which is incapable of free openness to the transcendental God." Congregation for the Doctrine of the Faith *Letter to the Bishops of the Catholic Church n Some Aspects of Christian Meditation*, no. 3. Oct. 15, 1989.

27 This example is taken from an outstanding article by Father Armand Nigro, S.J., *Prayer: A Personal Response to God's Presence*. The brief article is a tremendously helpful tool to put in the hands of anyone who wants to grow in a daily habit of relational prayer.

28 *Catechism of the Catholic Church*, no. 301.

29 Cf. Jn 10:30; 12:49; 14:9-11.

30 Jean Corbon, *The Wellspring of Worship* (San Francisco, Ignatius, 2005), p. 37.

31 See the "Contemplation to Attain the Love of God," in *The Spiritual Exercises of St. Ignatius*, nos. 230-237.

32 Cf. Eph 4:11-16.

33 Broom Tree Retreat Center in the Diocese of Sioux Falls. http://broom-tree.org/

34 St. Ignatius Loyola, *Spiritual Exercises*, n.317. Translation from Timothy Gallagher, *Discernment of Spirits, An Ignatian Guide for Everyday Living*, p. 8.

35 I strongly recommend Father Gallagher's *Discernment of Spirits, an Ignatian Guide for Everyday Living* (New York, Crossroad) as a thorough and outstanding introduction to the discernment of spirits.

36 Cf. 2 Cor 11:24-29.

37 *Catechism of the Catholic Church*, no. 2729.

38 *Catechism of the Catholic Church*, no. 2643.

39 See, James Keating, "Contemplative Homiletics", *Homiletic and Pastoral Review* (April, 2011).

40 From the Rules for Discernment of Spirits: "The fourteenth: likewise he conducts himself as a leader, intent upon conquering and robbing what he desires. For, just as a captain and leader of an army in the field, pitching his camp and exploring the fortifications and defenses of a stronghold, attacks it at the weakest point, in the same way the enemy of human nature, roving about, looks in turn at all our theological, cardinal, and moral virtues; and where he finds us weakest and most in need for our eternal salvation, there he attacks us and attempts to take us." St. Ignatius, *Spiritual Exercises*, n. 327. English Translation, Gallagher, *Discernment*, p.9.

41 "By reason of their dignity and mission, Christian parents have the specific responsibility of educating their children in prayer, introducing them to the gradual discovery of the mystery of God and to personal dialogue with him." Blessed John Paul II, *Familiaris Consortio*, no. 60.

42 See Deacon James Keating's *Spousal Prayer: A Way to Marital Happiness* (Omaha: IPF Publications, 2013).

43 "The concrete example and living witness of parents is fundamental and irreplaceable in educating their children to pray. Only by praying together with their children can a father and mother — exercising their royal priesthood — penetrate the innermost depths of their children's hearts and leave an impression that future events in their lives will not be able to efface." Ibid.

44 See the following articles by James Keating: "Teaching Parishioners How to Pray" *Homiletic and Pastoral Review* (June, 2010); "The Contemplative Pastor" *The Priest* (June, 2007); "What's God Doing in Your Classroom?" *Envoy* (Jan./Feb. 2009): 32-36.

45 See *WRAP Yourself in Scripture* by Karen L. Dwyer and Lawrence A. Dwyer. Omaha, NE: IPF Publications, 2011; *Prayer: A Personal Response to God's Presence* by Armand M. Nigro, S.J., and with John F. Christensen, S.J., *Praying with Scripture*. Jersey City, N.J.: Program to Adapt the Spiritual Exercises, 1960.

46 St. Ignatius Loyola, *Spiritual Exercises*, no. 75.

47 Second Vatican Council, *Gaudium et Spes*, no. 19, 1.

48 Blessed John Paul II, *Familiaris Consortio*, no. 62.

49 Ibid.

50 Pope Benedict XVI, General Audience, May 4, 2011.